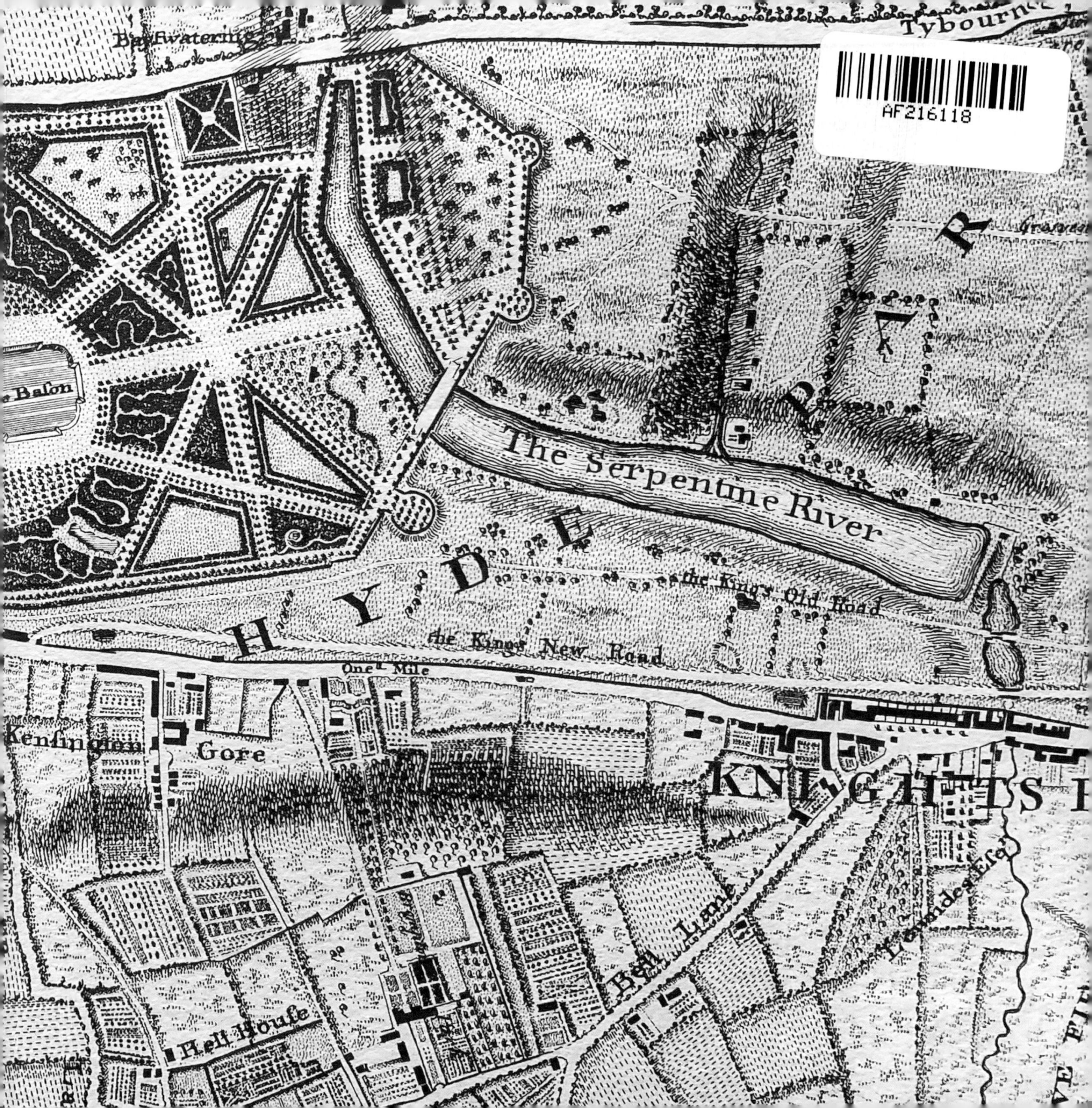

WILD ABOUT
Kensington

THE ROYAL LONDON BOROUGH

By Andrew Wilson

History Consultant,
Caroline MacMillan

Sponsored By

riverstoneliving.com

150 Years
JOHN D WOOD & CO.
London, Country & International Property

In memory of my lovely springer spaniel, Josie, who
sadly passed away during the making of this book, aged 17.

Welcome to Wild about Kensington

Welcome to the latest book in my London series of village books, my 26th so far. I was attracted to Kensington for a variety of reasons. As my book explores, its an area packed with fascinating places and lots of history but it's also where the husband of my historian has connections, so, it seemed an obvious choice. We started back in the autumn of 2022 and this will be the 7th book that Caroline and I have worked on together. Sadly, during this time, she has become ill and I have had to finish the book on my own.

As with all my books, it couldn't be done without a massive amount of help. I have mentioned a few of these people throughout the book, but I would like to single out one or two for a special mention. There is of course, Caroline, who I have mentioned above and I wish her well. I had to do rather more research on this book than normal, so, I'd like to mention how useful Wikipedia has become to me and because of that, I imagine I have become one of those rare people who actually makes a donation to them. What a fabulous resource it is. Then there are my sponsors of course, RiverstoneLiving and John D Wood & Co, who have been great. In the last two years, the costs of producing a book like mine have sky rocketed, so, their help has been invaluable. There is also a friend of my wife's, Clifford Gundle, who lives near Kensington and enjoys my work, who kindly made a very generous donation towards the book. This was very sweet of him and I hope he enjoys what I've done.

I am very passionate about my photography and make a great effort to be in the right place at the right time to take the very best picture I can. I am an inveterate weather watcher and I have it said on numerous occasions that the sun is always shining in my books. I hope you enjoy my latest foray into the people and places of our wonderful city and I hope to see you again soon.

Andrew Wilson September 2024

Below: My lovely springer spaniel, Josie, who sadly passed away during the making of this book, having reached the grand old age of 17. Knowing that she might not make it through to the end, I took her up to Kensington Gardens one Sunday in March 2023. **Right:** A rather fancy gate in Kensington Court.

Contents

A short history of Kensington

by Caroline MacMillan and Andrew Wilson

As with many places in London, the first real evidence you discover of a place's existence is the Domesday Book of 1086. In the case of Kensington, the book mentions the manor of Chenesitone, which, in the Anglo-Saxon language, means homestead or settlement. It is not until 1396 and a mention of trespass in some law papers that you find something better resembling the name, Kesyngton.

William the Conqueror, who was responsible of the Domesday Book, invaded England in 1066 and in taking over the entire country he gave much of the land to those who had sailed with him from Normandie. One of those supporters was Aubrey de Vere, Earl of Oxford and he was granted extensive land in and around Kensington and for many centuries was one of the largest land owners. His name lives on in the local street names, De Vere Gardens for instance.

Kensington was still very rural when in 1536 Henry VIII turned Hyde Park, which back then also included all of Kensington Gardens, into his own private hunting

The spectacular view of Kensington Gardens from the Min Jiang restaurant from the top of the Royal Garden Hotel.

Kensington is known for its mews. On the right, Pembroke Mews and on the far right, Kensington Court Mews. Please turn to page 106 for some more.

ground. He had acquired the manor of Hyde from Westminster Abbey, hence the name. It was enclosed as a deer park and remained a private hunting ground until James I permitted limited access.

One of James's supporters, Sir Baptist Hicks, built Campden House in 1550 (see page 120) which was then still heath and gravel land. His was a large estate, stretching from what is now Notting Hill Gate to High Street Kensington.

Another of James's circle, Sir Walter Cope, who had made his name during the reign of Queen Elizabeth I as one of

Lord Burghley's secretaries, also became a local landowner. In 1605, west of Campden House, he built himself a grand house, Cope Castle. Subsequently inherited by his daughter, Isabel, Countess of Holland, his castle became known as Holland House.

Still the domain of a few large estates, it was not until William and Mary came to the throne in 1689 that things started to change. William suffered from asthma and his wife decided it would be healthier for him to live away from the city and the Thames.

Now and Then: Kensington High Street 1893 and today (old picture courtesy of Francis Frith)

A short history of Kensington

Right: Northcliffe House, part of the old Barkers Building, is the home of the Daily Mail group of papers, which have long been associated with the area. Since their sale, it also accommodates the offices of the newspapers owned by Evgeny Lebedev, The Independent and Evening Standard & his TV station, London Live.

Their search brought them to a two storey mansion, Nottingham House, near the small village of Kensington, which was renamed Kensington Palace. For the next 70 years, the Palace became the principle residence of the monarchy and with its royal neighbour, the area became much more popular with many large houses being built.

It was here that wealthy people invested their money and bought a house where they could live during the week and go home to their stately homes in the country at weekends.

By the early 1800s several houses were built, Bute House now lies beneath Queen Elizabeth College and Aubrey House, originally built in 1698, is still occupied by the family who own it. This and Holland House, remain the only tangible evidence of the large houses that used to be here.

Kensington covers a large area, spreading from the north of the borough, from what is now Holland Park Avenue, to in the south, the Cromwell Road, Kensington Palace in east and to the boundary of Hammersmith in the west. It was not until the coming of the railways, that more substantial changes occurred. The large estates were broken up and developers moved in.

With the Royal connection, Kensington was still a place favoured by the wealthy and its new homes reflected this. It has many squares, among them Kensington Square and Cornwall Gardens, with one of the more attractive ones being Edwardes Square, tucked away behind Kensington High Street (all covered later in the book).

Above left: Queen Victoria memorial, Warwick Gardens. **Right:** Campden Houses in Peel Street; built in the 1870's by the National Dwellings Society, these seven blocks are still owned primarily by the council as social housing.

Right: For those of a certain vintage, including your author, will have visited Kensington Market at some stage in their lives. From its hey day in the 60's and 70's, it went the way of many places and finally closed in 2000. Their building was demolished in 2001 and is now a Currys (old picture courtesy of Wikipedia)

With the wealthy residents, came the local amenities to help provide for them. This became centred around Kensington High Street. When the tube arrived in the mid 1800's, the area soon became one of the most attractive shopping centres in London. This continued until the dark times of the 1970's when the large department stores started to be broken up.

Kensington still remains a wonderful place to live, if a little pricey for the average person, and with more local heritage than most other London areas.

Andrew Wilson and Caroline MacMillan

Right: A fascinating picture from the late 1860's, when The Albert Hall was under construction. The huge building in the background is the glasshouse in the gardens that the RHS used to have here, now the home of The Science Museum. (picture by kind permission from the Abbert Hal.

Above left: Kensington Vestry Hall, now Melli Bank. Completed in 1852, this was where the parish leaders used to meet.
Right: one of the lost pubs of Kensington. The Arms in Abingdon Road, first appeared around 1830 and sadly, permanently closed in 2009.

7

Kensington Palace

In 1605 the Palace started life as the two-storey Nottingham House. Shortly after William and Mary came to the throne in 1689, they bought the property from the Earl of Nottingham. Whitehall Palace wasn't suitable as their residence on health grounds, because William suffered from bad health and the residence was too close to the river. They then engaged Sir Christopher Wren, Surveyor of the King's Works, too vastly expand the property.

For the next 70 years, Kensington Palace was the favoured royal residence, with George II being the last royal to reside there, where he died in 1760. From then on, it was used by minor Royals, which continues to this day.

Above left: the statue outside the Palace of William III. **Right:** the Palace from 1724.

Autumn

The look and feel of the Palace gardens today is mainly down to the wife of George II, Queen Caroline, who engaged a designer and enclosed 300 acres of land from what was then Hyde Park. There is a stone statue with an urn on top (right) at the eastern end of The Serpentine that commemorates Queen Caroline and all that she did for the park.

Winter

The Palace is open all year round, so you can still visit in the depths of Winter.

Spring

The sunken garden (picture opposite) was created at the instigation of Edward VII in 1908. Diana, Princess of Wales was very fond of the garden and to mark the 20th anniversary of her death in 2017, the garden was upgraded. At the same time, a new statue was commissioned by her two sons, William and Harry and it now sits proudly at the eastern end.

The Orangery (top) was built in 1704/05 by Queen Anne. It became a popular venue for her summer parties and even today, you can hire the space for something special of your own. One of the architects that Anne commissioned to help her was no less a figure than Sir Christopher Wren. Sadly, the row of trees have gone since this picture was taken, April 2016, to make way for the new visitor experience, The Pavilion Restaurant.

Summer

The beautiful wild flower meadow that can be seen throughout the summer, was conceived in the autumn of 2018. The ground was ploughed to remove much of the grass and its seed, which can throttle wild flowers and the seeds were sown in April 2019. Since then the show has been magnificent and a wonderful space for a great variety of insects.

Kensington Gardens

The Gardens, once the private domain of Kensington Palace, is one of London's major Royal Parks. Located at the western end of Hyde Park, from which they were originally taken, the Gardens cover an area of 265 acres.

Queen Anne started the landscaping, which included the Round Pond and it was Queen Caroline, wife of George II, who requested that it be formally separated from Hyde Park in 1728.

Now and Then: the Round Pond at the turn of the last century and today.

Physical Energy by G F Mills, was unveiled in 1907.

Autumn

In 1731, as part of the landscaping, the Serpentine was created by damming the eastern outflow of the River Westbourne. The part of the lake that lies within Kensington Gardens is called The Long Water, pictured below. The bandstand, pictured on the right, was being renovated during the making of this book.

Winter

The Albert Memorial in Kensington Gardens, pictured opposite, was commissioned by Queen Victoria in memory of her husband. It took 10 years to complete, was paid for through public subscription and was opened in 1872 by Victoria, with Albert taking up his seat in 1876.

The Round Pond was one of the additions made by George II in 1730 and is surprisingly deep reaching depths of 5 meters in places. It has been popular with model boat enthusiasts and is in fact the home of the Model Yacht Sailing Association, which formed as far back as 1876. It is also popular with birds and swans in particular, which the public love to feed, despite protestations by the park not too. A black swan was present during the spring of 2023, as I compiled this book, which was lovely. Migratory birds can also be spotted during the winter, a Gadwall bottom right. Nothing is sacrosanct, even my camera bag, bottom right.

Above: another view of 'Physical Energy', which was erected in the park in 1907.

Opposite: Prince Albert was an enthusiastic gardener. The Italian Gardens at the northern end of The Long Water, were his idea and after his death, Queen Victoria completed it. On your way to the gardens on the west side of the Long Water, you pass a statue to Peter Pan (opposite top middle). J.M.Barrie's book was partly inspired by the gardens and the statue was commissioned by Barrie in secret and without permission and erected in 1912.

Spring

Bottom: there are two contemporary Serpentine Galleries in the park, separated by The Serpentine Bridge. Serpentine South, below, opened in 1970, and replaced what was once a tearoom. Events take place throughout the year and are free to enter (see page 166 for a picture of Serpentine North).

Overleaf: the beautiful Flower Walk.

Top: there are 22 gateways into Kensington Gardens but none more impressive than The Queen's Gate, which sits on the southern end of the park, opposite Queen's Gate.

Summer

The summer of 2024 was not as hot as that of 2022, when the Garden's resembled the Savannah, as shown right and below (compare to the same time this year, 2024, and see the difference in the colour of the grass, below right). One of the new and welcome innovations for the round pond in 2023 has been the introduction of a shingle island (opposite bottom), which the birds love as an escape from the people and the dogs. It even had a couple of pairs of coots nesting on it during the summer of 2024. **Bottom left & opposite top left & middle:** The Serpentine Gallery and exhibits.

Street Scenes

As highlighted by the recent pandemic, where would we be without our local shops and Kensington is no different. Once, one the most popular shopping destinations in London, Kensington lost some of its glamour when the large department stores shut their doors from the 1970's onwards.

From 2023, local businesses have had a new champion, an organisation called **'Opportunity Kensington'** (www.opportunitykensington.co.uk) who over the next 5 years will be investing £5 million locally to help the whole community; businesses, residents, employees and visitors. One of their first initiatives was to introduce Token; a local loyalty scheme designed exclusively for those who work, live or do business in Kensington, allowing them to make the most of discounted retail, cultural and dining experiences on their doorstep. Its easy to enrol - just visit their website from your mobile and download the App. They have also introduced a couple of wardens to help businesses and shoppers alike.

With greater things to come, its still down to us to support our local shops, as they need us now more than ever.

Then & Now: Kensington High Street around 1900 and 2023 (picture by kind permission of The Royal Borough of Kensington & Chelsea Archives.)

Kensington High Street

Kensington High Street Is one of west London's most popular shopping streets. Sadly, past its heyday, the local council has made a lot of effort recently to improve its attractiveness to shoppers, additions like the removal of the railings for instance. The street is still dominated by the magnificent architecture of the Barkers and Derry & Toms buildings. Designed by in-house Barkers architect, Bernard George, in the art-deco style, they include some wonderful hyraglifics down their sides(right).

Barkers

In its retail heyday, pre and post World War II, Kensington High Street boasted 3 department stores. Barkers, Derry & Toms and Pontings. John Barker and James Whitehead opened a drapery store in 1870 and through rapid expansion, in less than 20 years they had swallowed up all their neighbours. By 1920, they had bought both Pontings (1907) and Derry & Toms, although they continued to run them as separate entities. The boom of the 1920's prompted them to reconsider their vast empire and the magnificent buildings you see today were planned, with Derry & Toms opening in 1933 and Barkers in 1958. In 1957, The House of Fraser bought the business and there started a period of rationalisation, with the closure of Pontings in 1971, Derry & Toms in 1973 and the slow reduction in space at Barkers, which finally closed in 2006.

Top right: the story of Kensington and Derry & Toms wouldn't be complete without mentioning the fashion brand Biba. Starting modestly in Abingdon Road, Biba hit the big time by taking over the Derry & Toms building in 1973. However, its success at the time soon wore off and by 1975 it was broken up. On the top of the Derry & Toms building is one of London's hidden gems, a rooftop garden. Once open to the public, it has recently re-opened as a private members club. One of the new occupants of the Derry building is The Japan House (above), the cultural home of Japan in London, where they hold free events and exhibitions. They also have a restaurant where you can enjoy authentic Japanese cuisine. Japan has always had strong ties with Kensington (the Kyoto Garden in Holland Park being just one) and this new attraction is a welcome addition to the local area.

Below: Now & Then - looking west from Kensington Court, opposite The Royal Garden Hotel. **Right:** old sign for the Electric Lighting Station in Kensington Court. Built in 1888, this is one of the earliest surviving electricity generating stations in London. The station was built for the newly developed Kensington Court. I am grateful to Katie from 'Look up London' for this illuminating information.

Above left: The Royal Garden Hotel. This new building was completed in 1965, replacing the previous Royal Palace Hotel, just prior to the football World Cup. Perfect timing, as they were honoured to host the official reception for the triumphant England team the following year.

Right: the only Michelin Starred restaurant in Kensington, Kitchen W8, can be found just off the High Street in Abingdon Road.

Below: High Street Kensington Tube station opened in 1867, as part of the Metropolitan District Railway, the predecessor of The District Line and London Underground. Through a major redevelopment in 1906, where amongst other things a shopping arcade was added, this upgrade to the station helped usher in a golden period for this part of town.

Right: Earls Terrace dates from 1810, is Grade II listed and backs onto Edwardes Square.

This page: The Design Museum at the western end of Kensington High Street, opposite the redeveloping Odeon site, moved to its current site in 2016. Founded in 1989 by Sir Terence Conran, the museum's vision as envisaged by Sir Terence, was to encourage a better understanding of design. Through a series of events throughout the year the museum works hard to open up design to a wider audience.

Opposite bottom: The Milestone is one of a handful of 5 star hotels in Kensington. The building is in fact 3 late Victorian homes that were joined in 1922. Their General Manager, Andrew Pike, has been in place over 17 years and is particularly proud of some of the schemes they have introduced to try and cut waste. They have removed 95% of single use plastics and installed a Food Waste Management System, They also work closely with the charitable sector; have raised over £1M for Great Ormond Street and regularly allow the hotel to be used by local organisations to raise valuable funds for their important work.

Halloween

Very much an American thing, over recent years Halloween has become more and more popular over here, with some residents in Kensington going all out to impress.
This page: clockwise from the top, Phillimore Gardens, Argyll Road, Argyll Road, Kensington Gate and Holland Street. **Opposite Page:** top right, Holland Street, and left and bottom, Upper Phillimore Gardens.

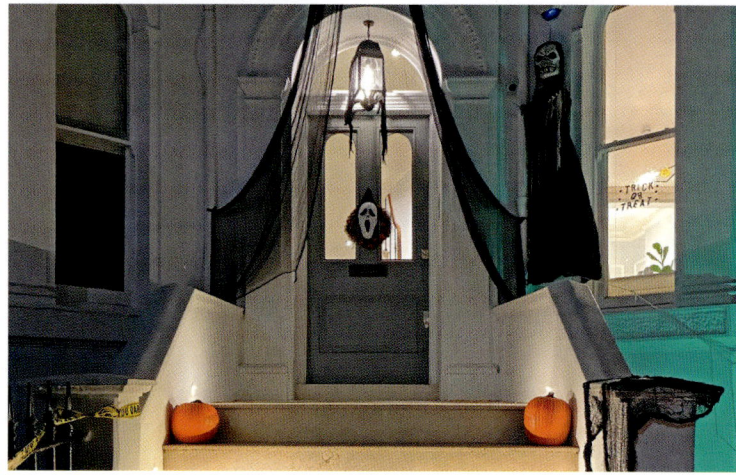

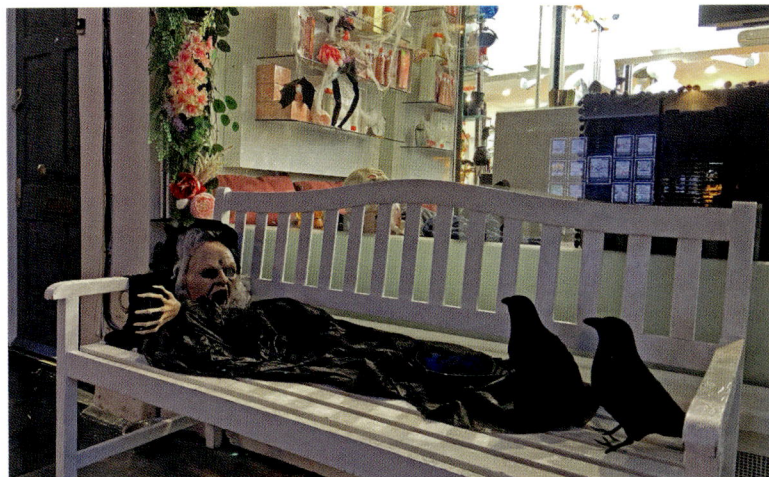

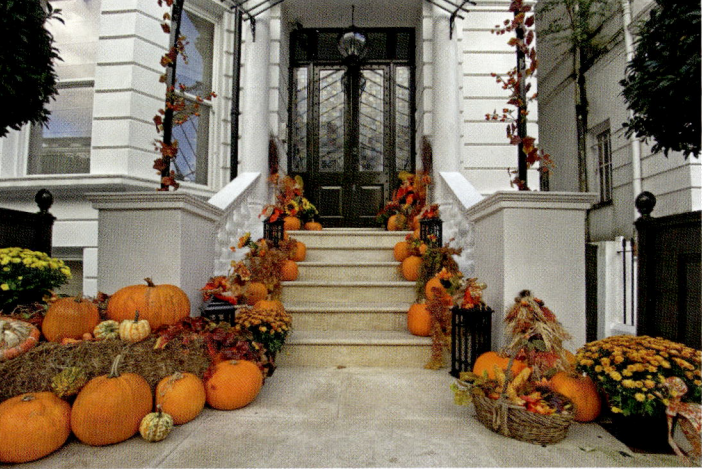

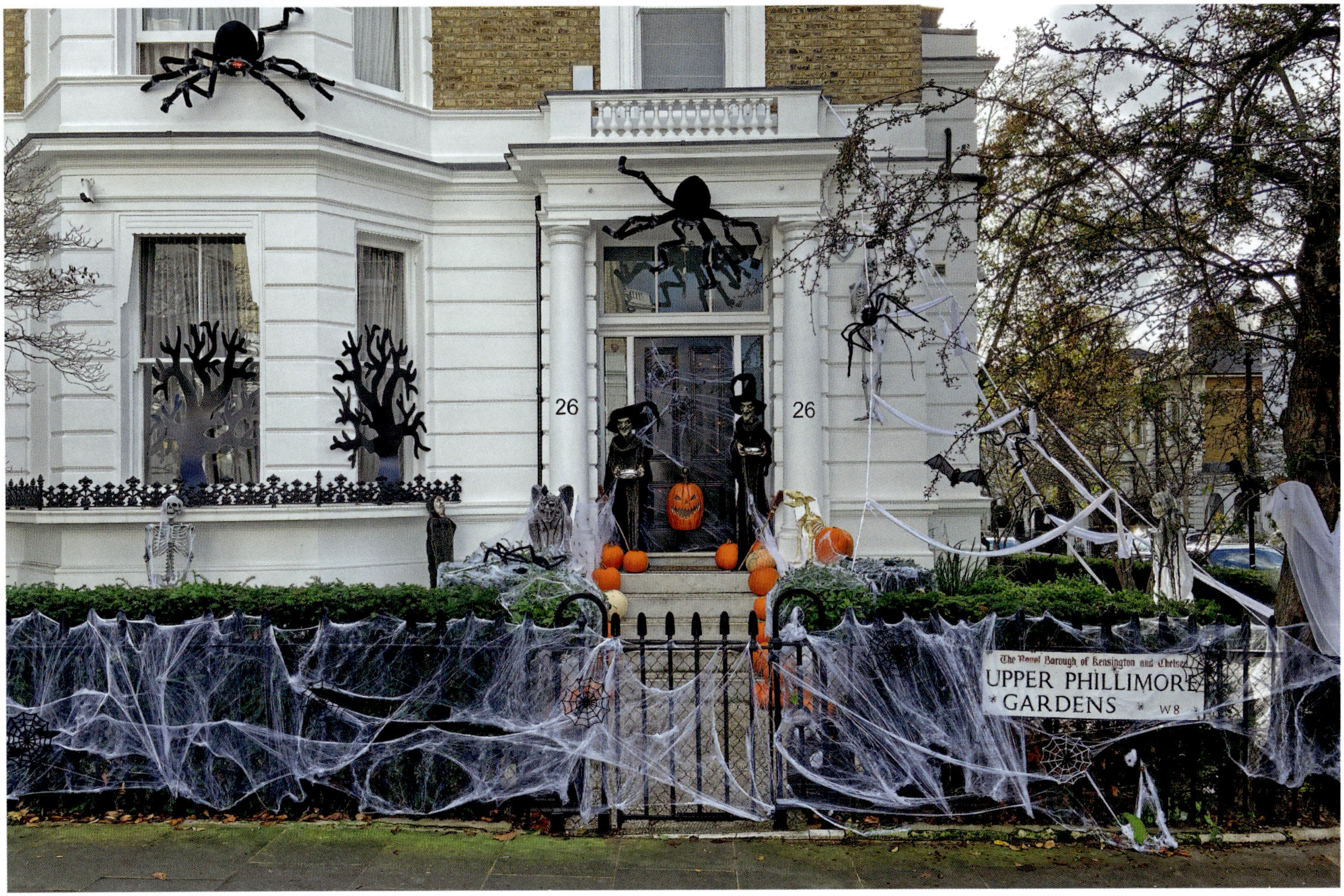
26
26
The Royal Borough of Kensington and Chelsea
UPPER PHILLIMORE
GARDENS
W8

Kensington Church Street

Traditionally known for its arts and antique shops, the southern part of street was formally known as Church Street and the northern end, Silver Street. At its southern end it is dominated by St Mary Abbots Church.

There has been a church here since the 12th century, with the current one dating from 1872. The picture right is of the previous church on the site before its demolition in 1869 (picture courtesy of Wikipedia). The spire is said to be the tallest in London.

The primary school at the back of the church dates from 1707, although the present buildings date from 1875. In the church yard you can look up and view the fun statues of a boy and a girl (below), which date from 1715.

If you have ever spied the sign 'ancient lights' on the side of a building (as here on the south side of the church) it relates to the years old law of your 'right to light'. There to protect citizens have an adequate level of light into their property.

Below: Kensington Church Walk runs between St Mary's and Holland Street and counts amongst its occupants Hornets Vintage Clothing shop and a rather smart mural at the southern end.

This page bottom: The bottom end of the street looking towards the High Street around 100 years ago and today.

Right: Kensington Lighting Company

Opposite top left: One of the more colourful shops in the street, Jimmie Martin and on the right, the lovely little terrier I spotted in the window of the shop next door, Reindeer Antiques.

Opposite bottom: The street has a sharp bend at the bottom, seen here in 1906 and as it is today (picture courtesy of Francis Frith).

This Page: John Daniel Wood founded the company of John D Wood & Co in London in 1872 at the age of just 23. The first premises were in Mount Street, Mayfair, opposite the Connaught Hotel. Now, over 150 years later the company has 30 offices across London, with one ideally placed at the north end of Kensington Church Street.

Opposite top left & right: Sally Clarke has been a feature of Church Street for almost exactly 40 years, first with her restaurant, which opened its doors in December 1984 and then her shop directly opposite. Still very much at the helm, Sally opened a third establishment, her bakery in Notting Hill, four years ago.

Above middle left & right: Another of the street's characters, I first met Tuggy from the Huntsworth Wine Company, when his shop was surrounded in scaffolding, as the building he was in was being renovated. Thankfully, in 2024 the scaffolding came down and he took the opportunity to refurbish the front of his store in a fabulous red finish.

Christmas

This page: clockwise from top left - Baglioni Hotel Kensington Road, Exhibition Road South Kensington, Argyll Road, Phillimore Gardens, Royal Garden Hotel and Upper Phillimore Gardens. **Opposite page:** clockwise from top left - High Street Kensington Station, Trotters Childrenswear Kensington High Street and the amazing Churchill Arms in Kensington Church Street..This famously colourful pub is managed by James, who kindly introduced me to several of Kensington Church Street's characters, including Sally and Tuggy.

TROTTERS

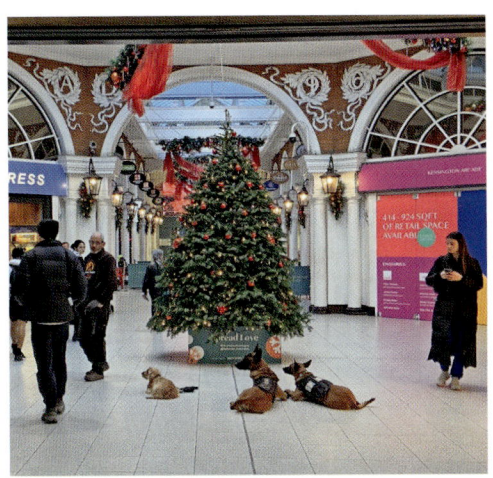

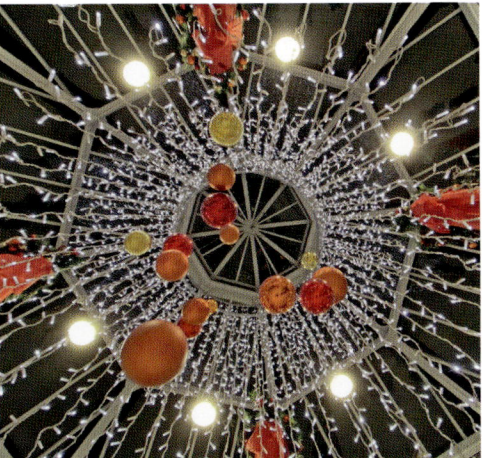

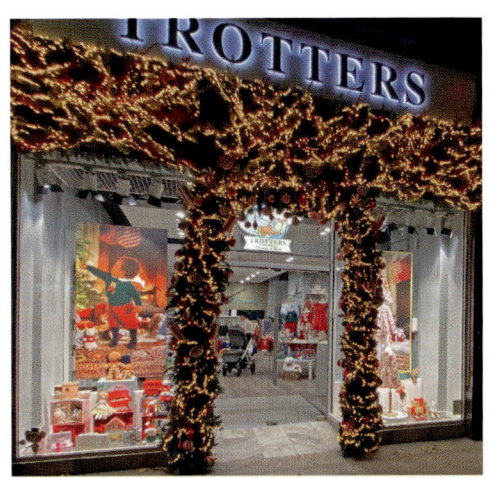

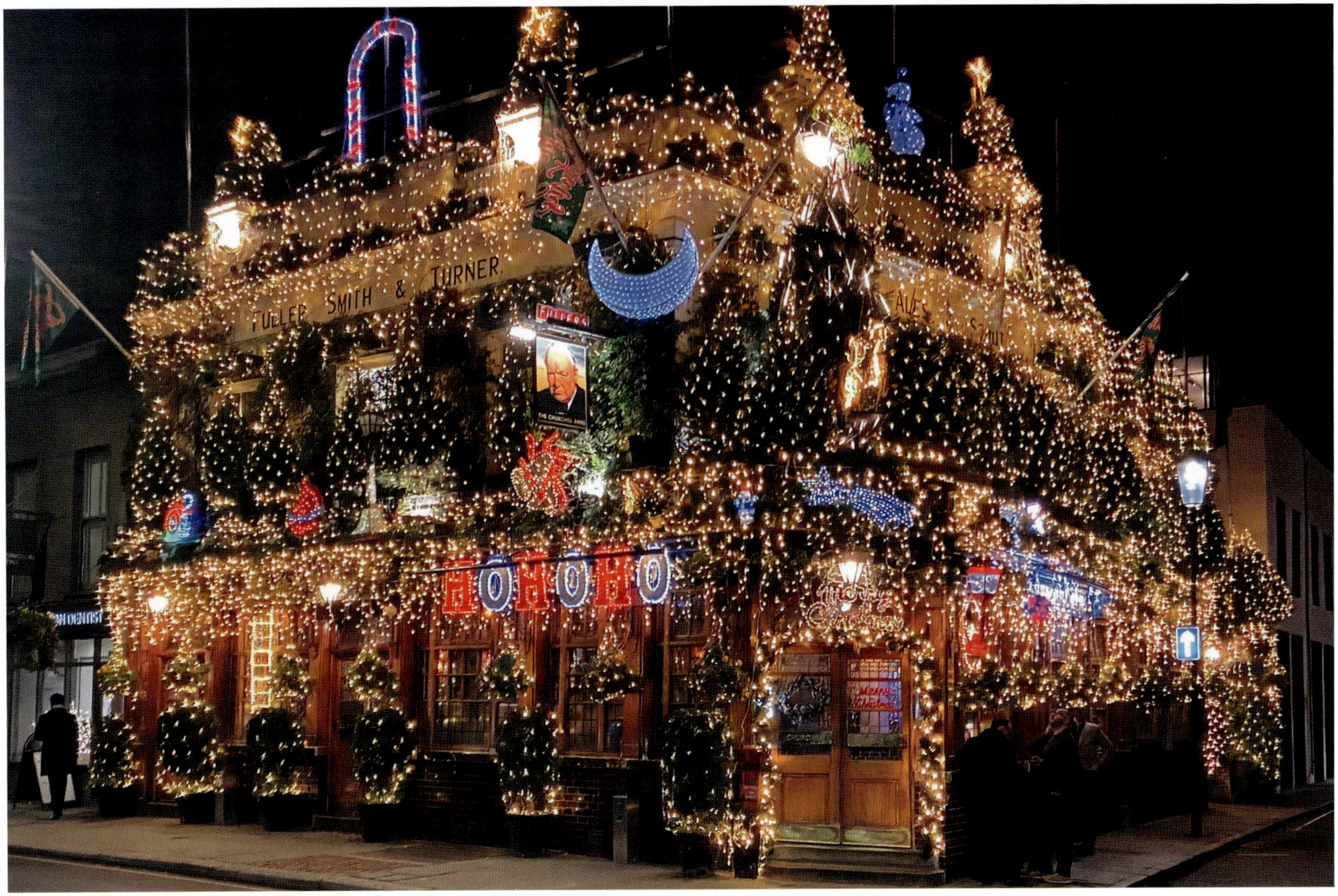
FULLER SMITH & TURNER
HOHOHO

Cornwall Gardens

As with much of London, the area now known as Cornwall Gardens was once a market garden. It was not until the middle of the 1800's that it started to be properly developed. The Gardens is a conservation area. Most of the houses around the Gardens are Grade II listed; the lovely Victorian postbox dates from 1860. It was kind of one of the residents to let me into the gardens one Saturday morning back in May 2023.

Edwardes Square

This pretty little square dates from 1811 and the gardens from 1820. I was fortunate that the garden participates in the excellent London Open Gardens weekend in June each year and I was able to gain a first hand experience of how well it looks. I see that one of its more notable residents was the funny man Frankie Howerd, who lived here from the 1960's until his death in 1992. Roger Bannister was also once a resident.

Spring comes to Kensington

This page: clockwise from the top - Argyll Road, Emperor's Gate, The Albert Memorial Kensington Gardens, Palace Gardens and Cottesmore Gardens.

Opposite page: clockwise from top left - Christ Church Victoria Road, Holland Street and Launceston Place.

Magnificent Magnolia

Spring is definitely on its way with the arrival of Magnolia and Kensington has some lovely examples.

This page: clockwise from the top right - Horton Street, Stanford Road, Argyll Road, Inverness Gardens and Kensington Gardens.

Opposite: clockwise from top left - Eldon Road, Phillimore Gardens, Victoria Road and Allen Street.

Gloucester Road

The road is named after Maria, Duchess of Gloucester and Edinburgh who had a house here in 1805. Formally called Hog Moore Lane, after the surrounding marshy area, the name was changed in 1850. The Gloucester Arms pub (below) dates from the 19th century and is Grade II listed. The Now and Then opposite top, is taken looking north from the Cromwell Road.

Bottom opposite: Gloucester Road becomes Palace Gate at its northern end, where can be found this rather impressive sculpture, Unfurl, which was commissioned by the local council and dates from the Millennium, and is by Eilís O'Connell.

Hyde Park Gate

Hyde Park Gate Is the name given to several adjoining roads at the boundary end of Kensington Gardens and off Kensington Road and is perhaps best known for being the residence of Sir Winston Churchill and where he died in 1965.

Beautiful Blossom

2023 was a wonderful year for blossom across Kensington, especially Brunswick Gardens, the main picture on this page, opposite and overleaf. I am grateful to Amanda Frame, the chair of The Kensington Society for the tip regarding the blossom and Brunswick Gardens in particular.

Right: York House Place. **Opposite top left:** Kensington Gardens. **Top right:** Gloucester Walk.

Top left: Inkerman Terrace. **Right:** Cornwall Gardens. **Above:** Phillimore Gardens.
Opposite page: top left and right: Inkerman Terrace. **Bottom:** Allen Street.

Kensington Square & Thackeray Street

The square dates from as long ago as 1695 and is the oldest such square in Kensington. The houses on the northern side, numbered 1-45, are Grade II listed. The square also contains no fewer than 4 blue plaques. It's interesting to note that English Heritage, who run the blue plaques scheme, which started in 1867, laid their 1,000th plaque just off the Strand in September 2023.

Bottom right: The Greyhound Pub can trace its history back to 1697, when there was a licensed premises here. It then became The Greyhound in 1710.

Opposite: as you pass old signs of the past (right), in the south eastern corner of the square is Thackeray Street, a charming red-bricked enclave full of little shops and cafes. It is named after the author of Vanity Fair, William Makepeace Thackeray, who used to live around the corner in Young Street.

Below top left: Sebastien's Hair Salon **Right:** Just off Thackeray Street, you'll find Ansdell Street and Skin 23.

Bottom right: Gallery 19 has been a feature of the area for over 27 years and is a real family affair. Sandra, who runs the shop, is married to a painter and their daughter is a photographer, and examples of their work can be found throughout the shop.

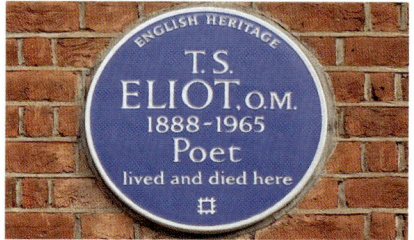

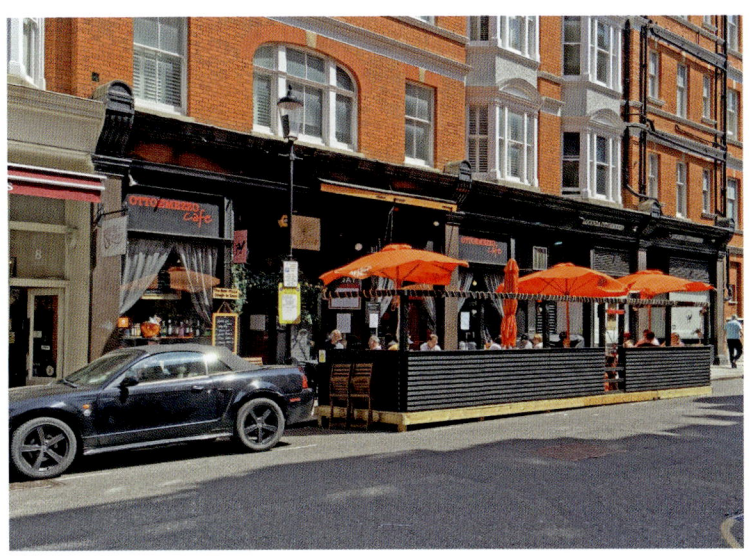

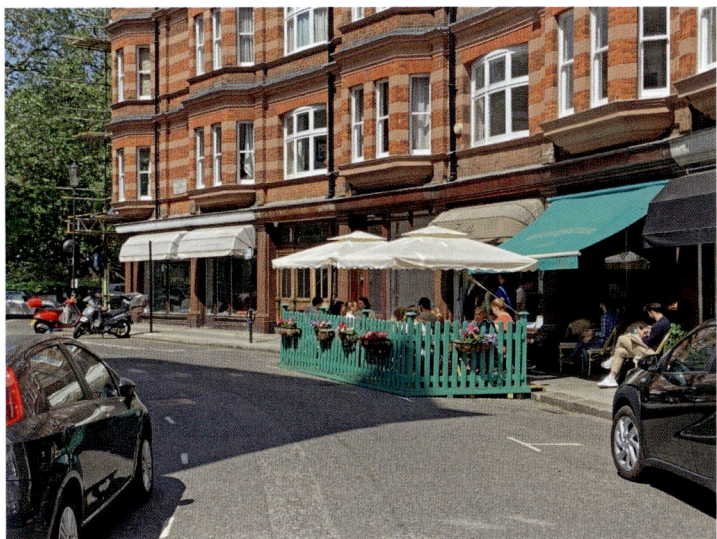

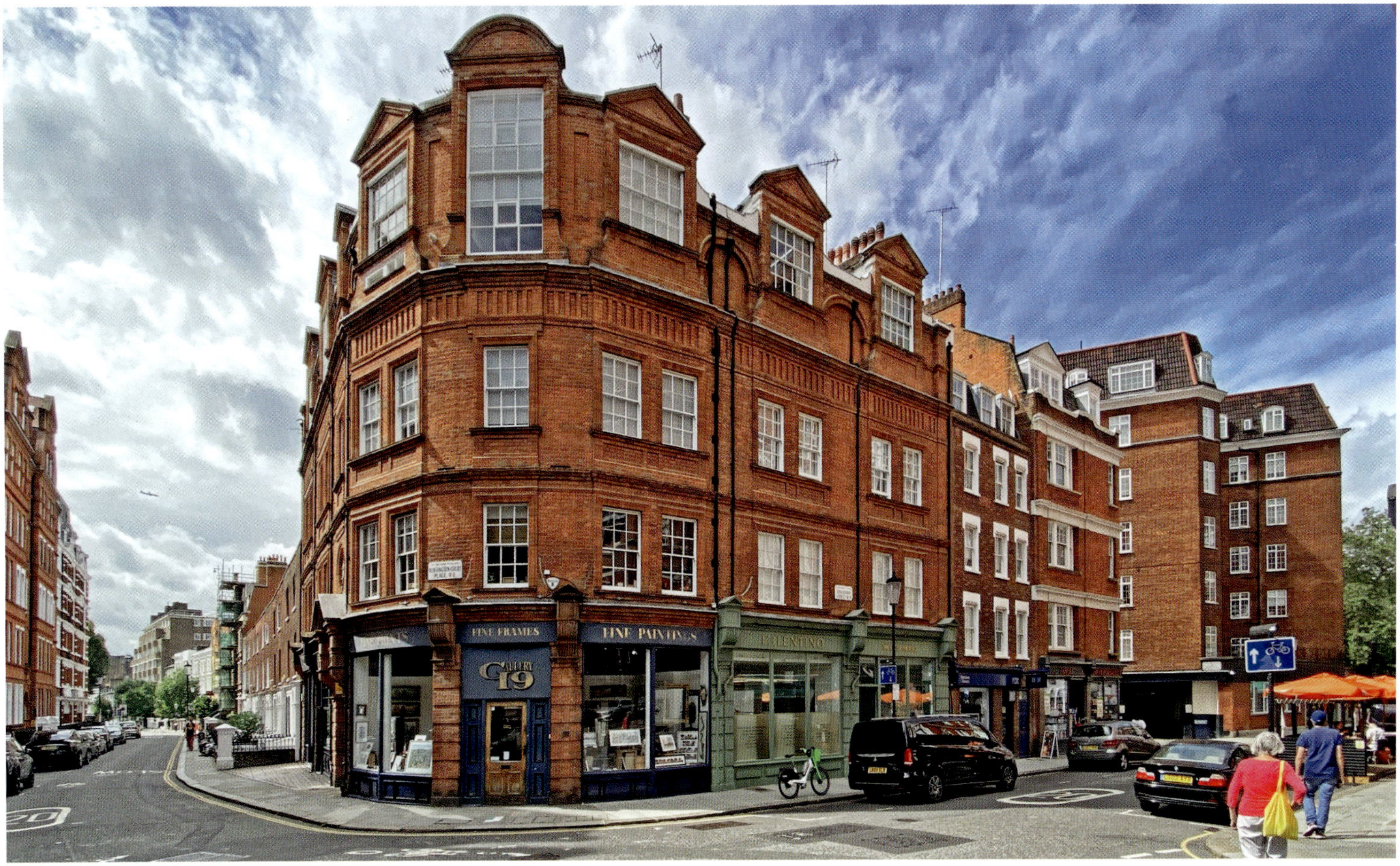
FINE FRAMES
FINE PAINTINGS
GALLERY 19

Lexham Gardens

Besides its traditional looking villas, much like many of the adjoining streets across Kensington, Lexham Gardens is notable in that as recently as 1989, a resident bought the freehold to the gardens found here. This farsighted purchase saved the gardens from being developed and continue to this day to provide a haven for its residents. Sir Cyril Taylor then engaged a garden designer to lay out the award winning gardens you see today, with its impressive looking horse and even a water feature.

Wonderful Wisteria

After the magnolia of March and the cherry blossom in April, comes the wisteria in May and quite a show it was in 2023.

This page top: Bedford Gardens. **Bottom left and right:** Abingdon Road. **Opposite page top left and bottom:** Bedford Gardens. **Right:** Victoria Grove.

BRIDGE
1879–1941
composer and musician
lived here

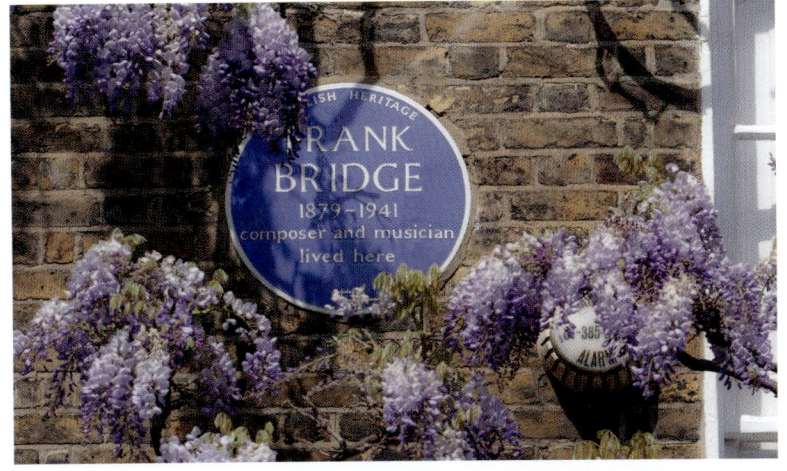

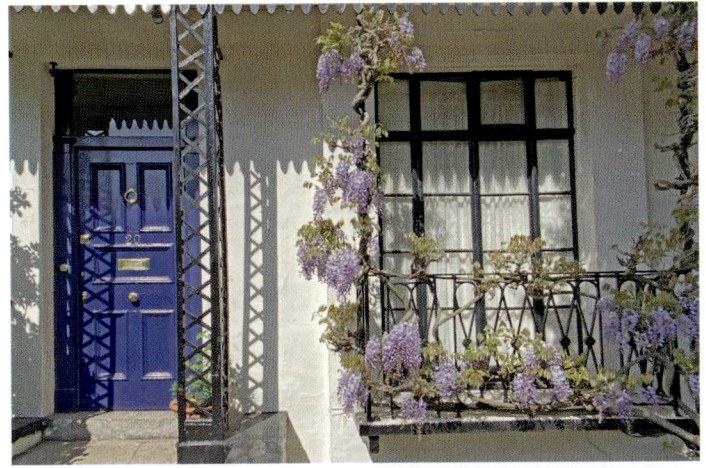

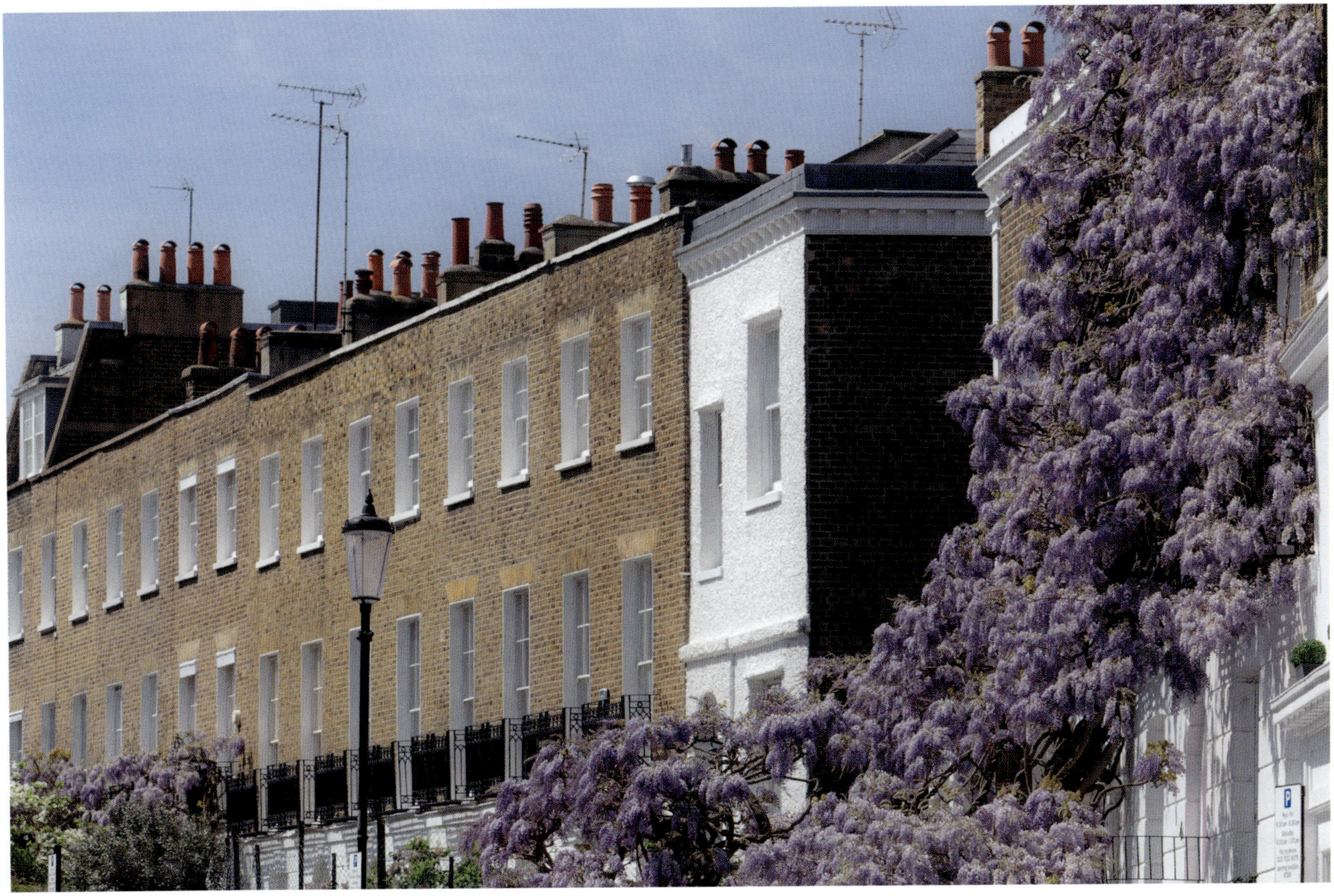

Opposite page: clockwise from top left - Brunswick Gardens, Sheffield Terrace and Agatha Christie's London home, Launceston Place and Pembroke Square. **This page:** Canning Place.

Coronation Day Street Parties

Best remembered for the truly awful weather that day, it's interesting to note it has been the case for all of the last five coronations. **This page top:** Abingdon Road and bottom, Kensington Road. The green cabbie shelter pictured is one of only 13 left in London. **Opposite page:** the street party held in Gloucester Road on Sunday 7ᵗʰ, when it was at least dry. Pictures of the distinctly wet party held in Hyde Park are at the back of the book.

This page: top 4 pictures, Holland Street. Bottom 2, Stafford Terrace.

This page: Pembroke Square and bottom right, M&S's rather fitting shop window in Kensington High Street .

Mews

Kensington is renowned for its beautiful mews. Once homes for horses, they are now fit for kings and queens.

Right: Radley Mews. **Below from the left:** Adam & Eve Mews, Cornwall South, Cornwall West. **Middle:** Drayson Mews, Elvaston Mews, Holland Park Mews.

Above: Osten Mews, Petersham Mews and Queens Gate Place Mews.

Clockwise from top left: Canning Place Mews, Lexham Mews, Atherstone Mews and Kynance Mews.

Queen's Gate

Built for The Great Exhibition, Queen's Gate opened in 1855. Formally called Albert Road, it changed to Queen's Gate in 1859. At the northern end of the road, near the actual gate to Kensington Gardens, is an equestrian statue of Field Marshal Robert Napier, 1st Baron Napier of Magdala, erected in 1920 (opposite top left).

Opposite page: Top left: Queen's Gate Place Mews.

Right and bottom: Queen's Gate Gardens.

Royal Albert Hall

Opened in 1871 by Queen Victoria, The Central Hall of Arts and Sciences, as it was originally conceived, was the idea of Prince Albert after the success of his Great Exhibition in 1851. He proposed that the area be home to a variety of permanent facilities for the public to enjoy. Although he died before realising his dream, some of the profits from the Great Exhibition were used in creating The Albert Hall, as it became to be known once Queen Victoria had lain the foundation stone in 1867. It is perhaps best known today as the home of the BBC Proms, which have been hosted here since 1941.

Warwick Road

The changing face of the western end of Kensington.

From the railway goods yard of old (see right), Warwick Road has in recent years seen some dramatic changes. Retirement villages are nothing new but modern methods are changing the way things used to be. We are all living, longer and healthier lives, and the new development from Riverstone, in West Kensington, offers people considering retirement something very new. As the development opened its doors last year, I was kindly invited in to take some pictures. (aerial photo by kind permission of Aerial Photos of Great Britain).

South Kensington

The area covered by South Kensington is bigger than you think and possibly deserves a book all of its own. With space at a premium and the museum area having its connections to royalty and Prince Albert in particular, I felt it important that we at least cover them.

As has been highlighted earlier in the book, after the success of the Great Exhibition in 1851, it was Prince Albert's wish that part of its legacy should see an area nearby to where in Hyde Park the event took place be given over to the arts and sciences. The exhibition took place roughly where the Albert Memorial is today. So, with some of the profits from the event, the commissioners of the exhibition bought an area of about 87 acres west of what is now Exhibition Road and set the ball in motion for what we find today. The V&A, the Science Museum, the Natural History Museum (opposite),

The Royal College of Music and Imperial College, to name but five, and all world renowned places of learning.

The opening of the tube line out west accelerated the changes to South Kensington from mostly market gardens to what you see today. The stations themselves, which opened in 1868, were upgraded by architect, Leslie Green, in the first decade of the last century. Things of beauty in their own right, they bear their architects distinctive hallmark of an ox-blood red terracotta facade and are Grade II listed.

Gloucester Road

South Kensington

The Natural History Museum, opposite, opened in 1881 and is recognised the world over as the pre-eminent centre of natural history and the research of related fields. It holds over 80 million items and is free to enter. Before work was started on their exterior gardens, they used to have a skating rink in their grounds at Christmas.

Of particular interest to your author, one of their major new initiatives is their Urban Nature Project, for which the exterior garden improvements form a part of and are due to open in 2024. They are working to give people across the UK the motivation and tools to safeguard nature in towns and cities, so that people and the planet can thrive. Hooray to all that.

The Victoria & Albert Museum (right), which was officially opened by Queen Victoria in June 1857, is the world's largest museum of applied arts, decorative arts and design. It houses a permanent collection of over 2.27 million objects. It was founded in 1852 and named after the Queen and Prince Albert.

Right: when South Kensington tube station was built (below), they rather cleverly added the wonderful tunnel you see today, to avoid visitors to the museums from having to cross the Cromwell Road.

Middle right: the statue to the Hungarian composer, Bela Bartok, which sits outside South Kensington Station and celebrates the fact that on his numerous visits to this country he would stay locally with friends.

Bottom: established in 1907, Imperial College London, focuses on the study of science, engineering, business, and medicine. Across a large campus off Exhibition Road, at its heart sits the impressive Queen's Tower.

Right: another of the more eminent organisations found off Exhibition Road, is the Royal Geographical Society. Formed in 1830, they moved to their present location in 1913. One of its many accolades has been the support of many of our famous explorers, one being Sir Ernest Shackleton, whose statue can be found on the side of their building.

Below: the exterior of The Victoria & Albert Museum on Cromwell Road.

The Great 2023 Exhibition Road Festival

The Festival is a free annual celebration of science and the arts held each summer in South Kensington. Led by Imperial College, they are joined by many of the local institutions and were blessed with some glorious weather in June this year.

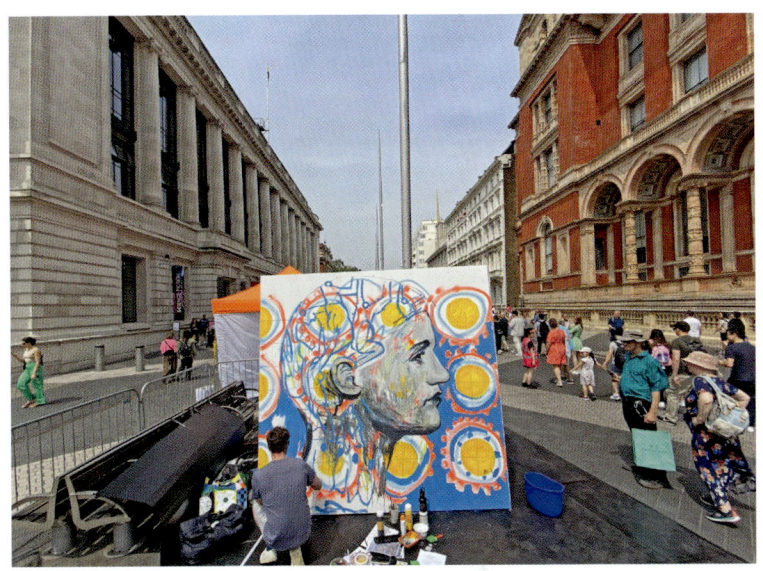

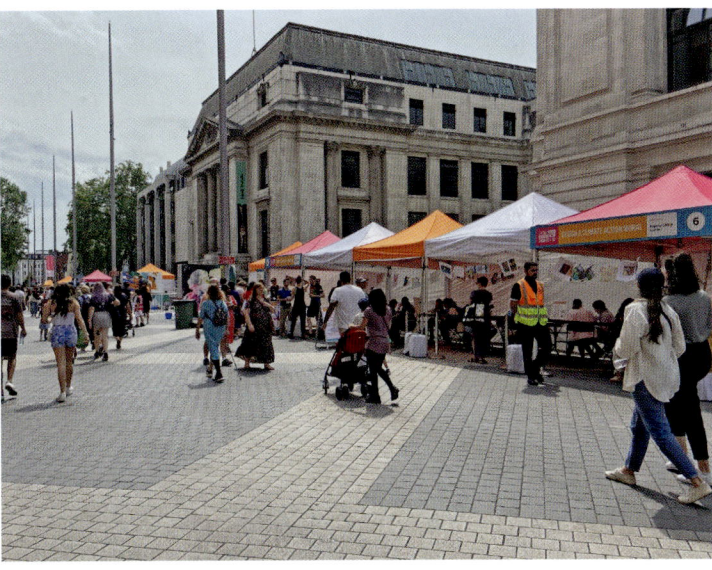

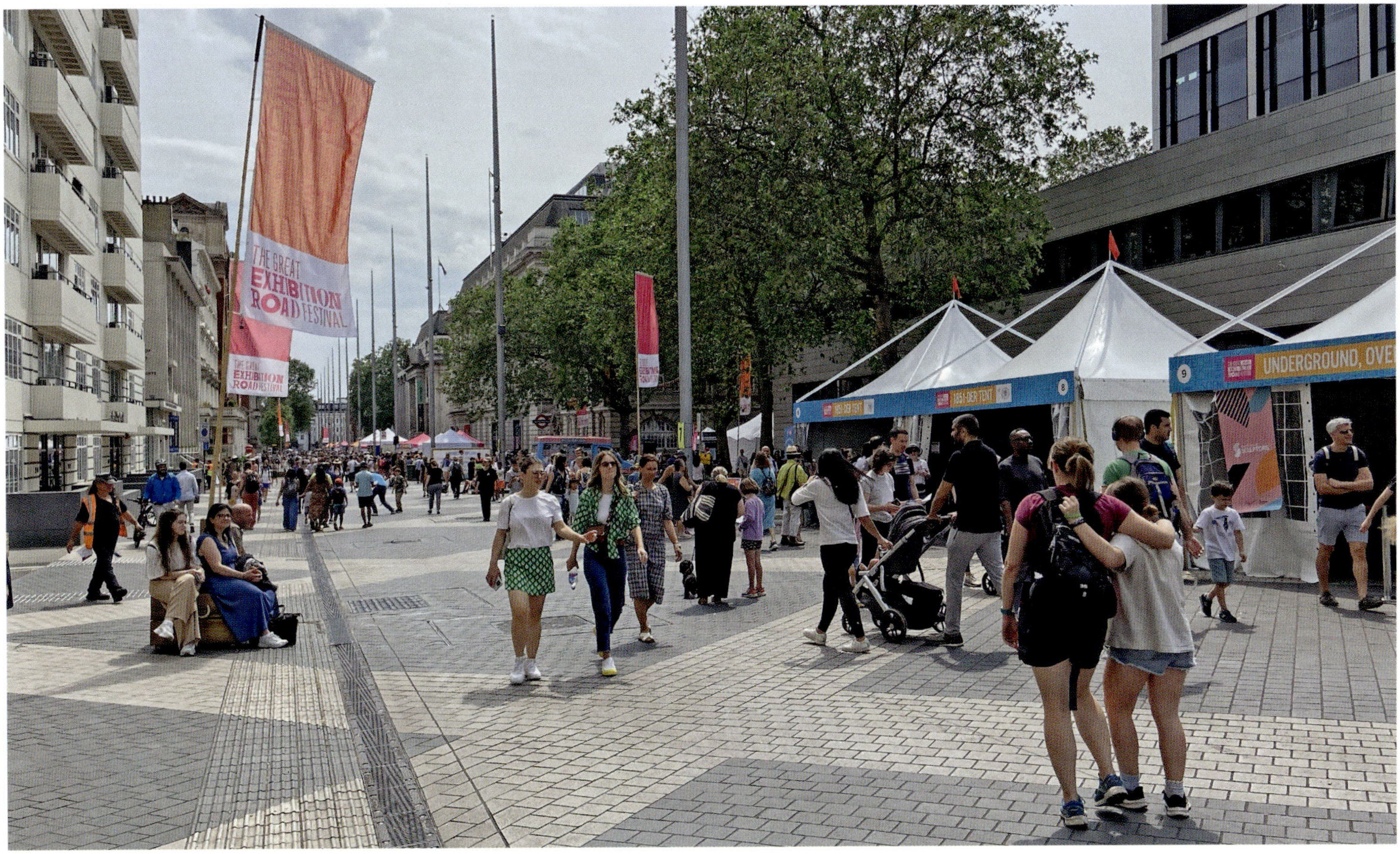
THE GREAT EXHIBITION ROAD FESTIVAL
UNDERGROUND,

Campden Hill

The area known as Campden Hill, runs north of Kensington High Street and is bordered on the other three sides by Holland Park in the west, Holland Park Avenue in the north and Kensington Church Street in the east.

It's named after Sir Baptist Hicks, 1st Viscount Campden, who was a successful cloth merchant and MP from the early 1600's. He had a large house here in Kensington, Campden House (below right, from 1720, from Wikipedia), which stood well into the 1800's and his country estate, which was in Campden, Gloucestershire. There is no trace of his house in Kensington today, but looking at old maps, it was situated on the corner of Gloucester Walk (Terrace as it was) and Kensington Church Street.

Alongside the lovely homes, the hill is dominated by Holland Park (see page 132). It is also nice to observe that some of the old estates live on, Phillimore for example, in the street names. Also, the reference to the Kensington Wells (see page 128) in the old John Rocque map on the inside cover of the book.

Above left: Campden Hill Road from early last century. **Opposite:** Observatory Gardens.

Below: it was nice to observe that when the new residence, Academy Gardens, was redeveloped they retained the old gates from the college that was once here.

Bottom Left: The Windsor Castle at the top of Campden Hill Road can trace its history back to 1820. **Bottom Right:** Campden Hill Court.

Right: as a photographer it would be remiss not to mention that the famous 20th Century photographer, Bill Brandt, lived at the top of the hill in Airlie Gardens.

Opposite top: Observatory Gardens is a rather beautiful row of houses, which as the blue plaque explains, are named after a local resident, who owned a large telescope back in the 1800's. After he died and the area was redeveloped, they retained the connection by naming it after him or rather his telescope.

Opposite Bottom: Campden Hill Gate, Duchess of Bedford's Walk.

ROYAL BOROUGH OF KENSINGTON AND CHELSEA

OBSERVATORY GARDENS

DERIVES ITS NAME FROM THE OBSERVATORY THAT
SIR JAMES SOUTH THE ASTRONOMER BUILT HERE
IN 1831 AND WHICH CONTAINED FOR A TIME
THE LARGEST TELESCOPE IN THE WORLD.
AFTER THE ASTRONOMER'S DEATH THE SITE
WAS SOLD TO THOMAS CAWLEY WHO BUILT
THE EXISTING HOUSES IN THE 1880'S.

Aubrey Walk

Aubrey Walk used to be known as Notting Hill Grove but was renamed in 1893. It used to be the approach to Aubrey House, that still exists behind the gates at the western end (right). Aubrey House is the last of the big houses that used to be here, Wycombe Lodge being just one of the lost ones.

The rather striking green towered church, is St George's. It was built by a local man, whose son George was its first vicar when it was consecrated in 1864.

Wycombe Square, on the south side of the street, is a smart new development, completed in 2004. Besides the new homes, as part of the plan, they also laid some new courts for the tennis club next door (overleaf).

Wycombe Square

127

Campden Hill Lawn Tennis Club

Whilst I was researching Campden Hill, I was fascinated to discover that their used to be a spring on top of the hill and that in the 1800's a reservoir was built, including a large tower (see below, the view up Campden Hill Gardens, as it was and is now). The tower was demolished in 1970. The tennis club started in 1884, partly over one of the reservoirs and was one of the first to open purely for tennis. Thames Water finally decided to sell their land for redevelopment and as part of the plan, the developer came up with an ingenious idea. He used one of the underground reservoirs (one was demolished in 1970) to extend the tennis club underground, leaving more space for their new home scheme above (see top right). As one of the highest points locally, during WWII an anti-aircraft gun was positioned on one of the courts. Thank you to the club for allowing me in to take these pictures.

Campden Hill Square

The Square was laid out in 1826 on land that was formerly a farm back in the 1600's called Stonehills. Originally called Notting Hill Square, the name was changed in 1893.

Hillgate Village

Hillgate Village, originally known as "The Racks" was part of the Campden House estate and came into the possession of the Phillimore family during the eighteenth century.

It has lately become known as the area with the beautiful coloured houses.

28

WELCOME TO FOX PRIMARY SCHOOL
PORTOBELLO ROAD
CORONET
LOVING LEARNING MAKING A DIFFERENCE

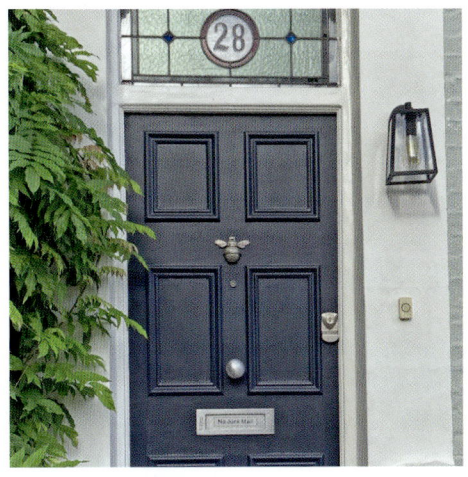

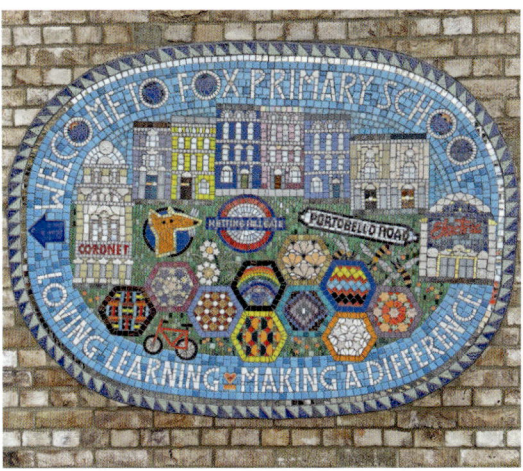

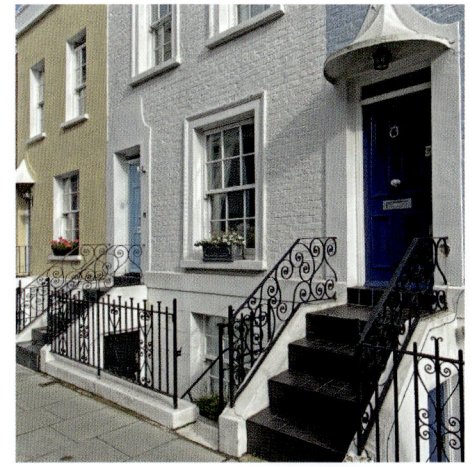

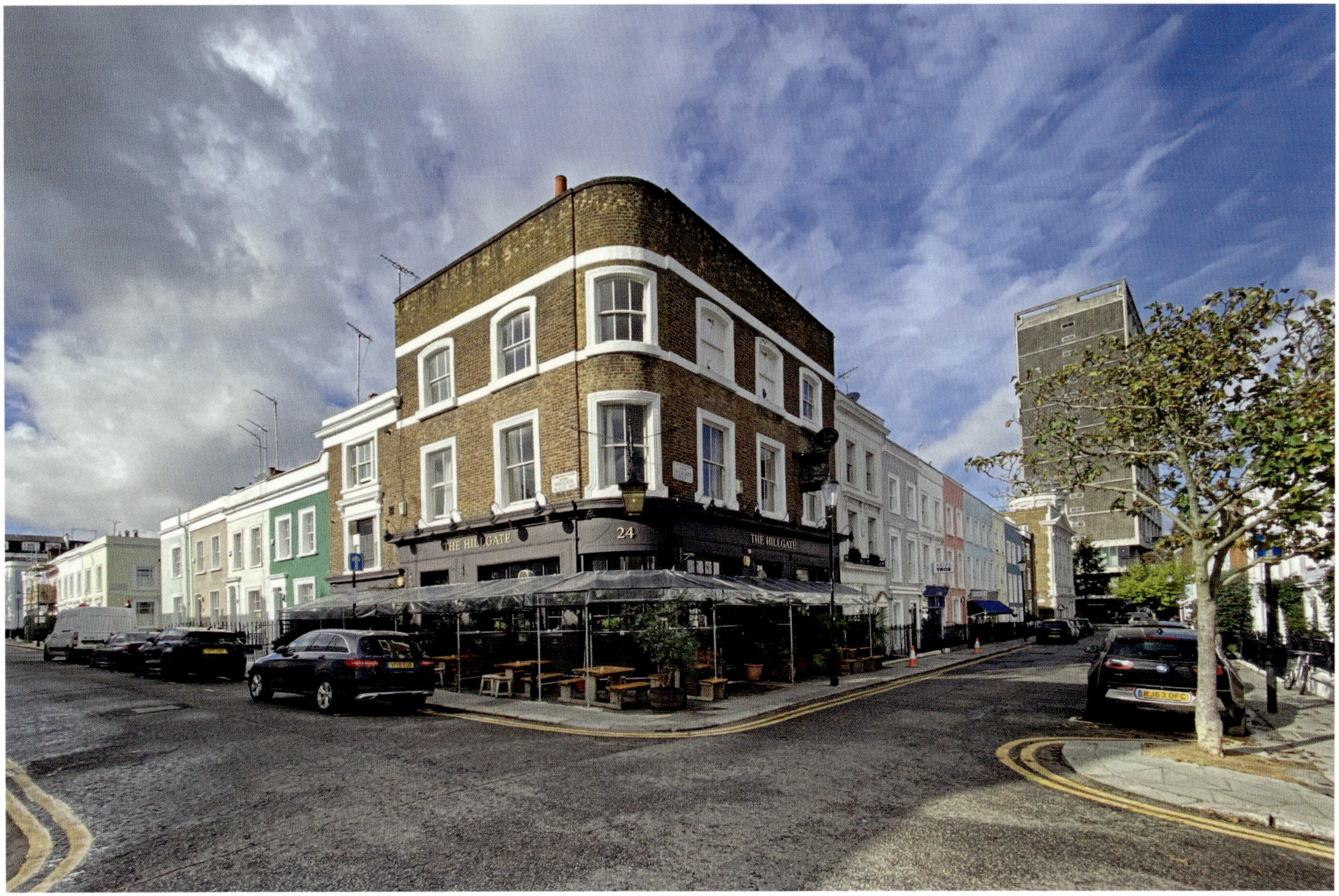
THE HILLGATE
24
THE HILLGATE

Hornton Street

As well as a fine set of houses, providing great photographic symmetry (opposite bottom), Hornton Street is also home to Kensington Town Hall. This new complex was commissioned in the rather brutalist fashion in 1965, when the two boroughs of Kensington & Chelsea amalgamated. Work was completed in 1976 and Princess Anne officially opened it in 1977. The fabulous piece of art in the middle is called Mars: War & Peace by Luke Jerram and was on display during July 2023.

Opposite top: Campden House Close, in Hornton Street, opposite Gloucester Walk. It was originally a mews.

Holland Park

Holland House was originally known as Cope House and the estate consisted of what is now the park. Together with Aubrey House they are the last remaining evidence of the large mansions that used to exist in the area. The house was built in 1605 by the diplomat Sir Walter Cope. The building later passed by marriage to Henry Rich, 1st Baron Kensington, 1st Earl of Holland.

During WWII, the house was badly damaged in an air raid and as can be seen from the picture below (dating from 1905) only parts of the house remain.

Over time, the house has been a centre for the political elite (early 19th century) and also the focus for the arts more generally, with many artists residing in the area. Further adding to this cultural heritage, Opera Holland Park was established in 1996, and continues to this day to produce award winning shows each summer.

Above left: these rather lovely murals, which can be found in the grounds, were commissioned by the Friends of Holland Park in 1994. Painted by Mao Ben Biao, they depict an imaginary scene from one of the garden parties that used to be held by the Earl of Ilchester in the grounds of the house in the 1870's. Old picture courtesy of Wikipedia.

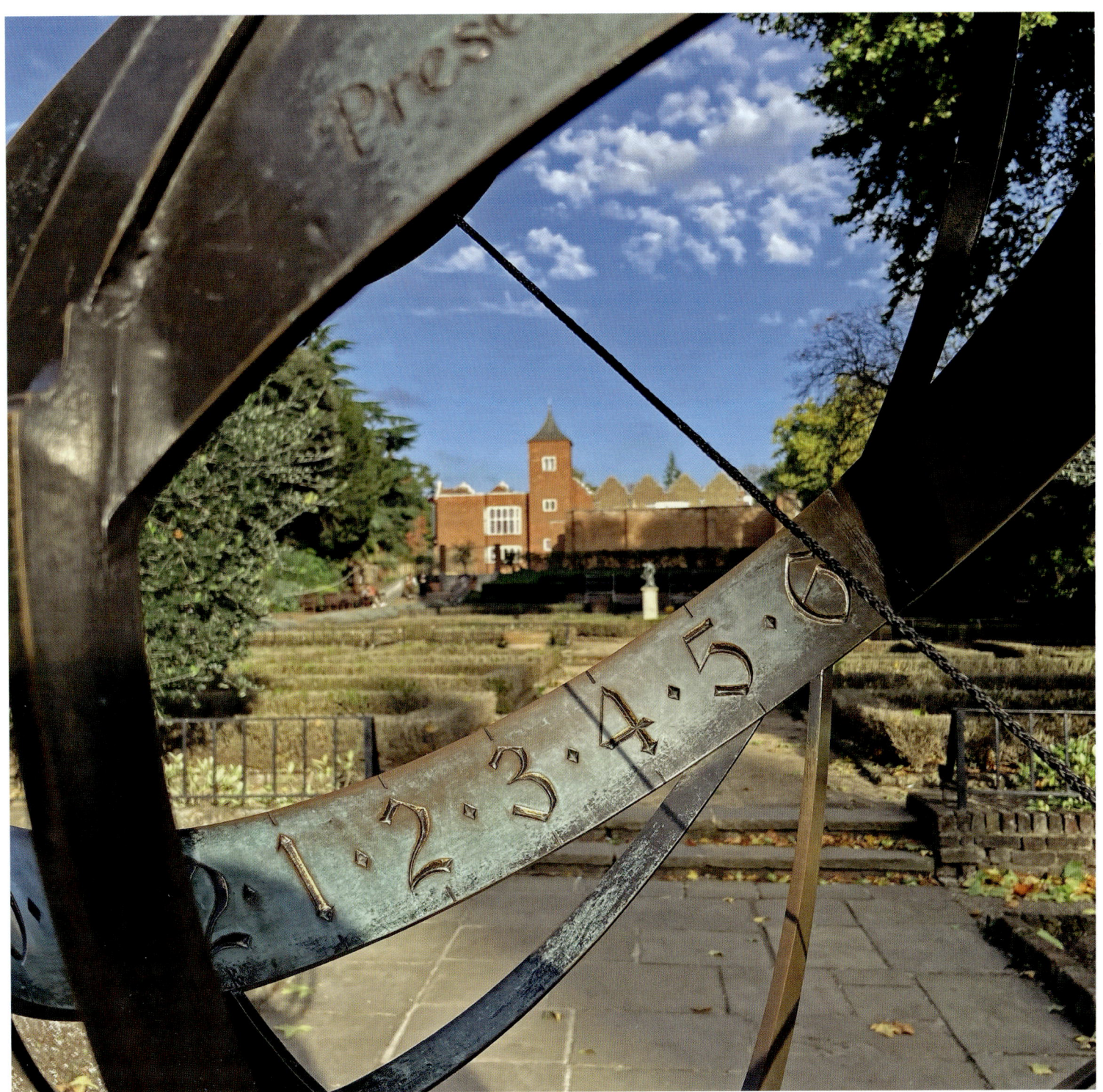

Autumn & Winter

At the beginning of the 20th century, Holland House had the largest private grounds of any house in London, including Buckingham Palace.

Overleaf left: The Kyoto Garden, which can look its best in autumn, was constructed in 1991 on the occasion of the centenary of the Japan Society in Britain. It was built by the Kyoto Chamber of Commerce and gifted to Kensington to commemorate the long lasting friendship between Japan and Great Britain.

Spring

Opposite bottom: The Kyoto Garden was opened by HRH Prince of Wales and by HIH The Crown Prince of Japan on 17th September 1991.

The previous page left: The Annunciation by Andrew Burton. **Right:** The Kyoto Garden

Summer

Over time, much of the estate of Holland House has been sold off for development but still covers over 50 acres.

When the paraphernalia of the opera season has gone, parts of the old building are exposed (right).

Hyde Park

The park, which covers 350 acres, was established by Henry VIII in 1536 when he took the land from Westminster Abbey and used it as a hunting ground. It opened to the public in 1637. As with Kensington Gardens, major improvements were made in the early 18th century under the direction of Queen Caroline.

In 1851, Prince Albert held his Great Exhibition in Hyde Park. As if pointing the way, over the years other statement events have continued to take place here. For instance, a series of free concerts back in the 60's and 70's. In more recent times, a regular series of large outdoor concerts takes place in the summer and before COVID the last night of the proms has extended its coverage by putting on a stage show in the park.

During the making of this book, the Queen's death and the Coronation of Charles III were marked by the household cavalry firing their guns in the park. The events were relayed to large screens in the park. It was a shame that the weather was so poor.

Then and now: The Serpentine today and at the turn of the last century.

Autumn

This page: to commemorate the life of Diana Princess of Wales, who used to live in Kensington Palace, a memorial fountain was opened in 2004. In keeping with her love of children, the public is encouraged to play in it. It can be found beside The Serpentine, on the south side between the Serpentine Bridge and the Lido.

Winter

It is rare that it snows in the centre of London these days, especially enough to settle. I was therefore very lucky that in December 2022, during a cold spell, it snowed very heavily and the park looked beautiful, at least for one day.

Right: Serenity, erected in 2009 and by the Lido was donated by Halcyon Gallery and the sculpture's creator, Simon Gudgeon, to help raise funds for the The LookOut Discovery Centre, in the Park. At the base of the sculpture you can see 1,000 plaques dedicated to supporters of the appeal.
The Centre's mission is to help introduce children of all ages to the wonders of the natural world.

Swimming

As far back as 1830, swimming and races in particular, have taken place in The Serpentine. The Serpentine Swimming Club, formed in 1864, is the oldest swimming club in Britain. They swim every day in the Lido area between 5:30 am and 9:30 am and also during a famous race on Christmas Day. In September each year, 100's take to the water in Swim Serpentine.

Spring

Hyde Park was a popular duelling spot during the 18th century, with 172 taking place, causing 63 deaths.

With the coming of spring, the birds in the park start to pair up and the males fight for the right to the females. When the swans start it can be quite something to witness.

Opposite: The Serpentine Gallery North. It is worth going around the back of the building, as you get to admire the large scale artwork up on the wall, by Atta Kwami.

Above: Great Crested Grebes are by far my favourite birds, with at least a couple of pairs on The Serpentine. Their mating ritual, where they pass each other weed is one of the wonders of the natural world in the UK. In summer of 2024, at least one of the pairs successfully bred, with two young spotted begging in September.

Summer

Whether its boating on The Serpentine, taking in a concert or just taking a relaxing stroll, Hyde Park is a wonderful way to escape the trials of life. There are also lots of cafes and places to sit so that you can enjoy the view in comfort.

Opposite: The Henry Moore Arch, which is actually in Kensington Gardens, as viewed from Hyde Park. It was given to the park by Moore in 1980. As can be seen, its not only the public that get to enjoy it.

Top Right: Norwegian War Memorial, which was presented to the people of Great Britain by The Norwegian Navy and Merchant Fleet 1978 as a thank you for our support during World War II.

Above Right: sadly, not the best picture but these birds, Reed Warblers, are very difficult to see let alone photograph. However, I was extremely pleased to hear one during one of my many visits to the park and tried my best to spot it. The reed bed by the Lido is not that big, so its lovely to think that even here they are happy to set up home. Reed Warblers are migratory birds, who come to these shores in summer to breed.

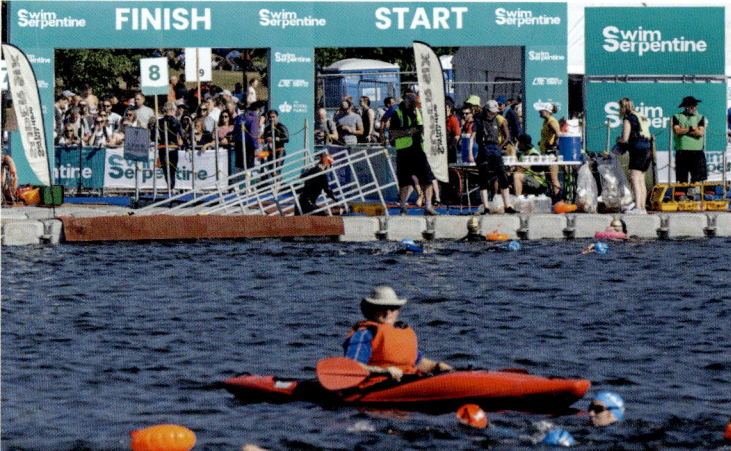

Swim Serpentine

In September each year, hundreds of open water swimmers take to the Serpentine for this charity event, which is run by the people that give us The London Marathon. The wildlife just looks on.

The Queens Funeral & The Coronation of King Charles III

The Royal Family are intimately associated with all things Kensington, so it was with great sadness that during the making of this book, The Queen died. As part of the funeral arrangements, The Household Cavalry, whose barracks are just off the park in South Carriage Drive fired their guns in the park. As with many large scale events, there was also a big screen erected in the park, for people to watch.

The Coronation of Charles III was a damp affair (as have the past 4 coronations been) but still people braved the awful conditions to party in the park (overleaf). The flypast had to be postponed due to the low cloud and only the Red Arrows flew. Thankfully, the flypast took place in June during Trooping the Colour, where the weather was kinder. The Memorial Flight was the highlight for me (above).

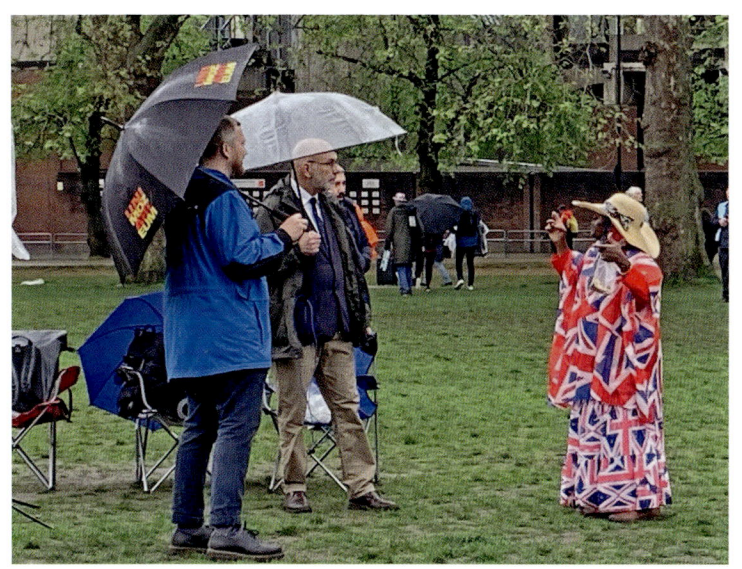

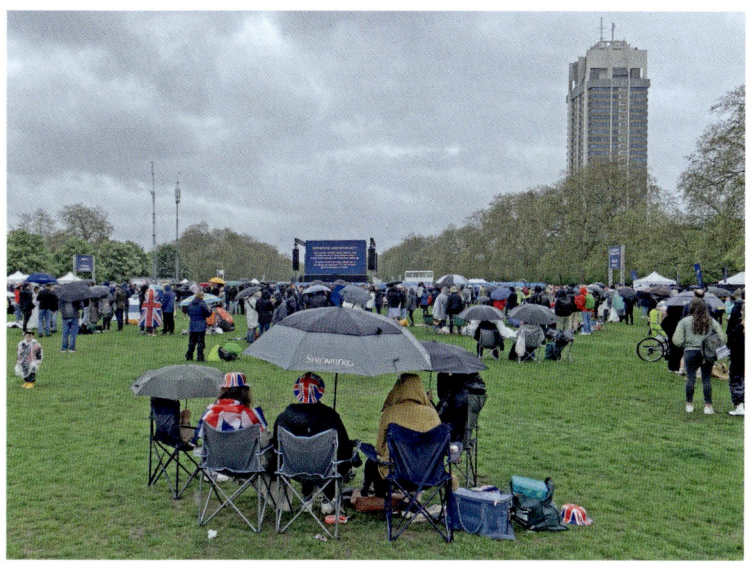

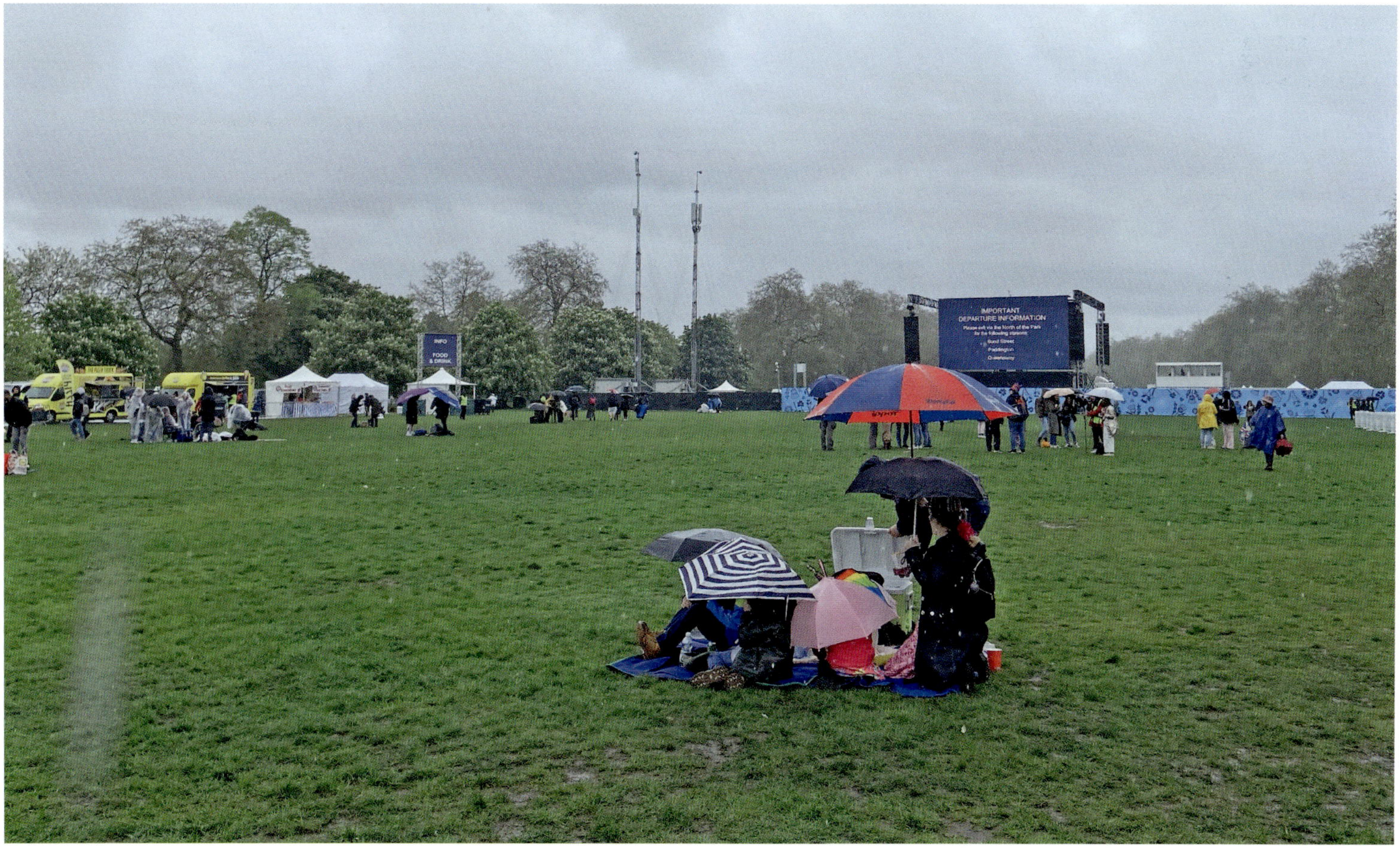
IMPORTANT
DEPARTURE INFORMATION

First Edition: © Unity Print & Publishing Limited 2024

History Consultant: Caroline MacMillan

Old Pictures: pages 54, 57, 68, 83, 112, 122 and 128 by kind permission of the RBKC Archives & Local Studies, Kensington Central Library, Phillimore Walk.

Old Pictures: By kind permission Francis Frith, Pages 5,58 and 69.

Printed by: Matsis Global Print Solutions, Turkey

Follow Andrew on X and Instagram @WildLondonPics

Colour Management: Paul Sherfield

Published by Unity Print & Publishing Limited, 18 Dungarvan Avenue, London SW15 5QU Tel: 020 8487 2199 - aw@unity-publishing.co.uk www.wildlondon.co.uk

Most of the pictures in this book were taken using a Canon 6D plus lenses with additional shots taken on an iPhone 11

Picture left: Balloons over The Serpentine.

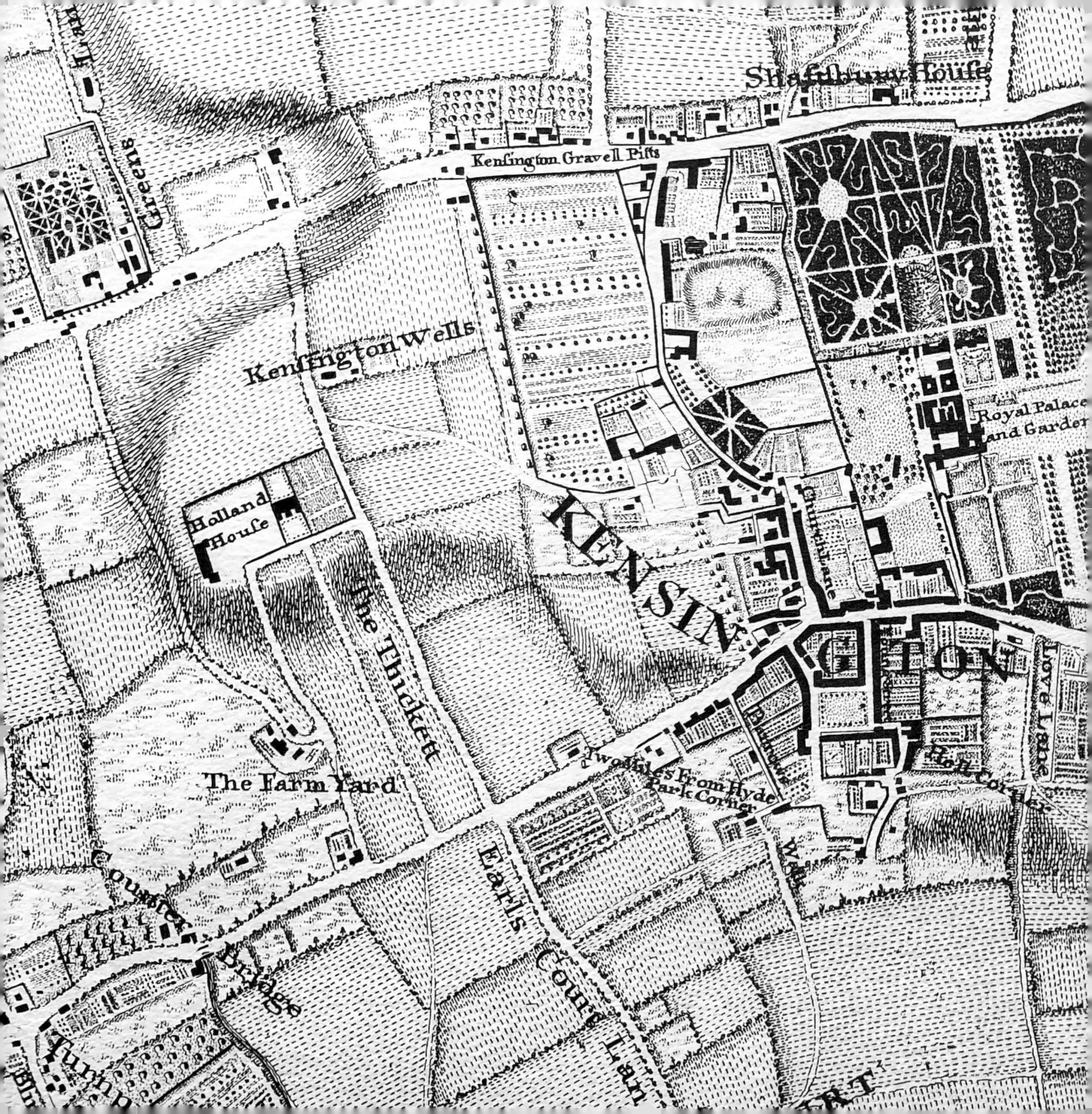

Shaftsbury House

Kensington Gravell Pitts

Greens

Kensington Wells

Royal Palace
and Garden

Holland
House

KENSI

The Thicket

Church Lane

TON

The Farm Yard

Two Miles From Hyde
Park Corner

Holl corner

Earls Court Lane

Walk

Court

Bridge

Lane